3

Germs are in the water.

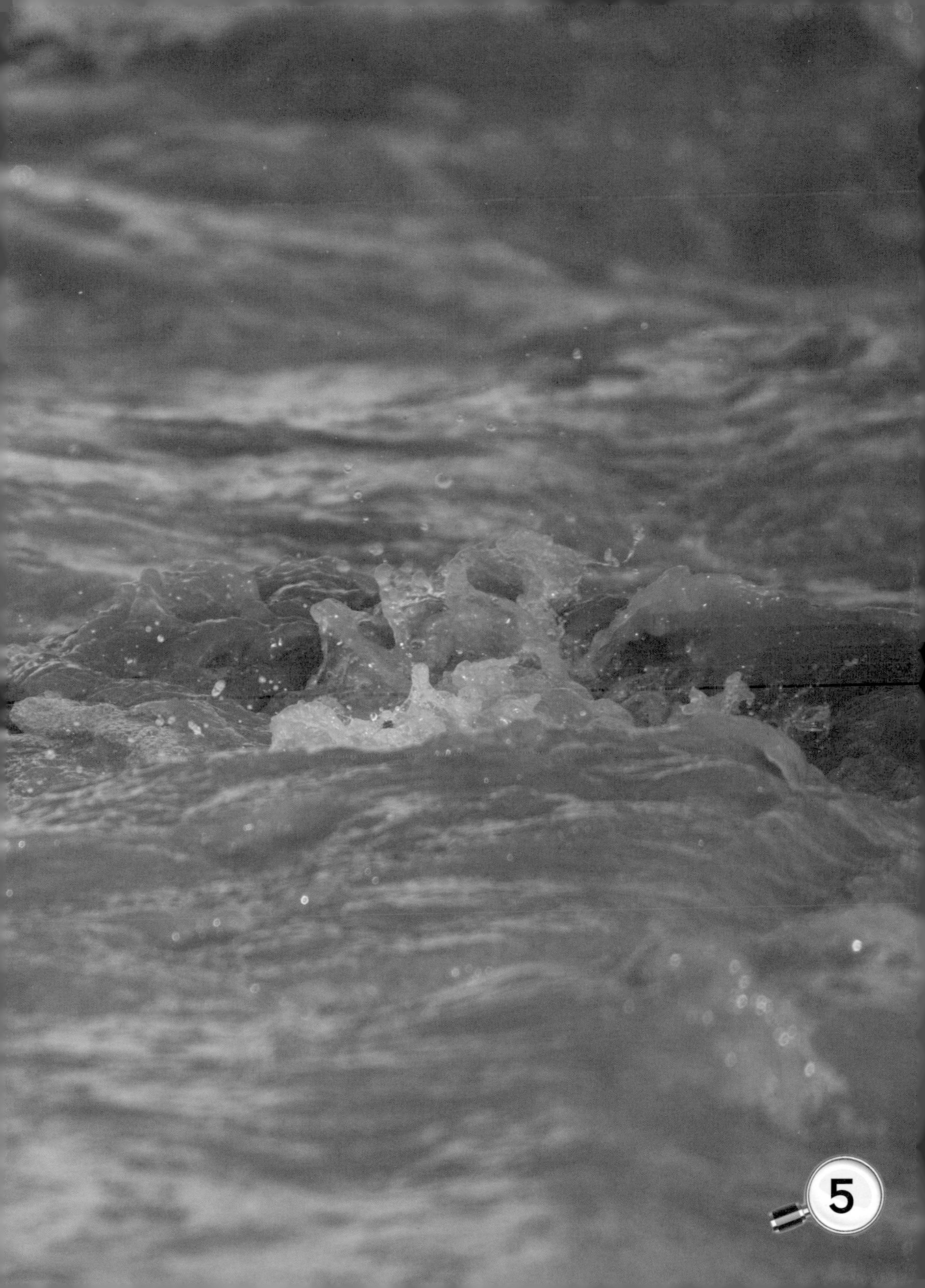

Germs are on me, too!

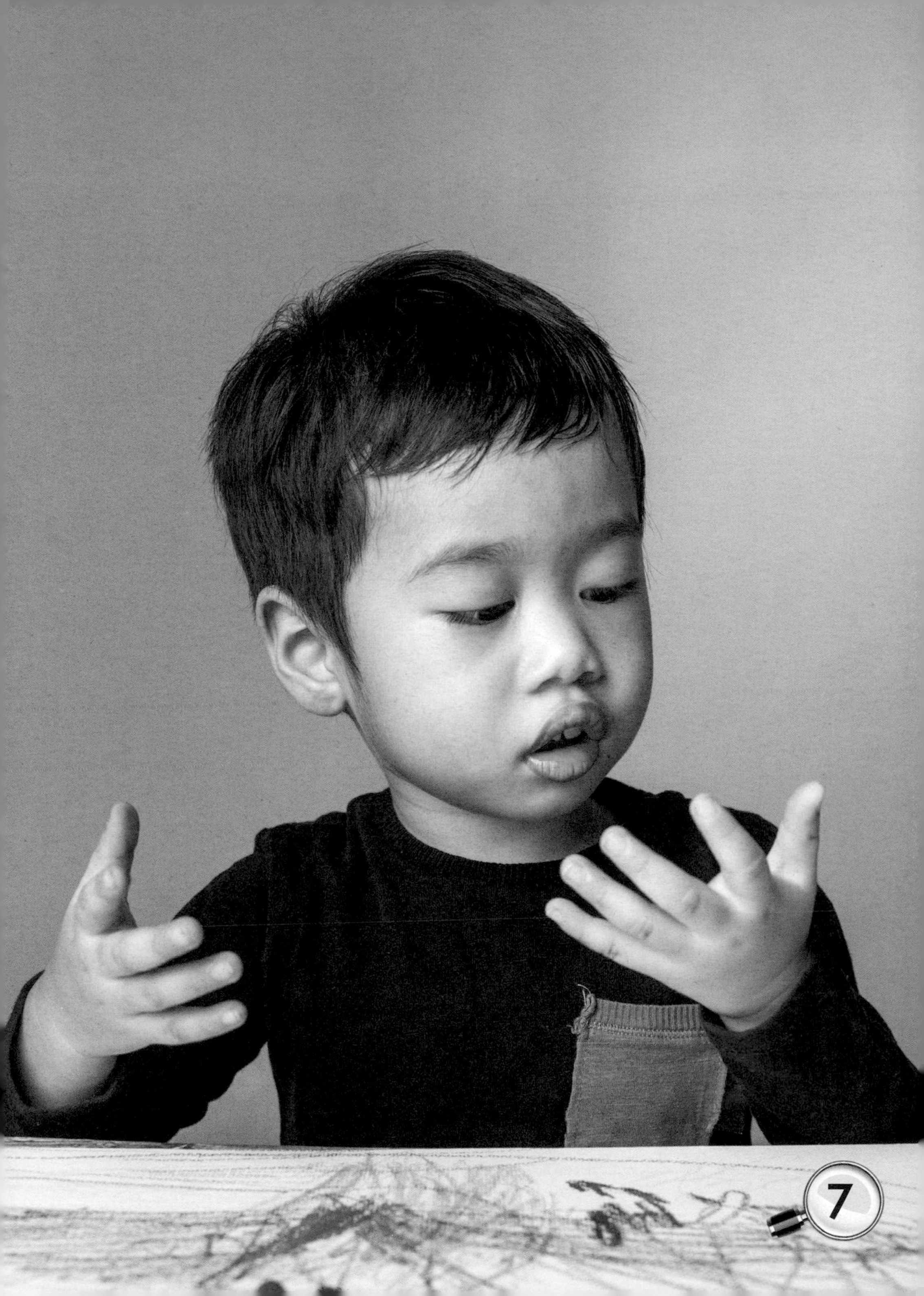

Germs can make
my mom **sick**.

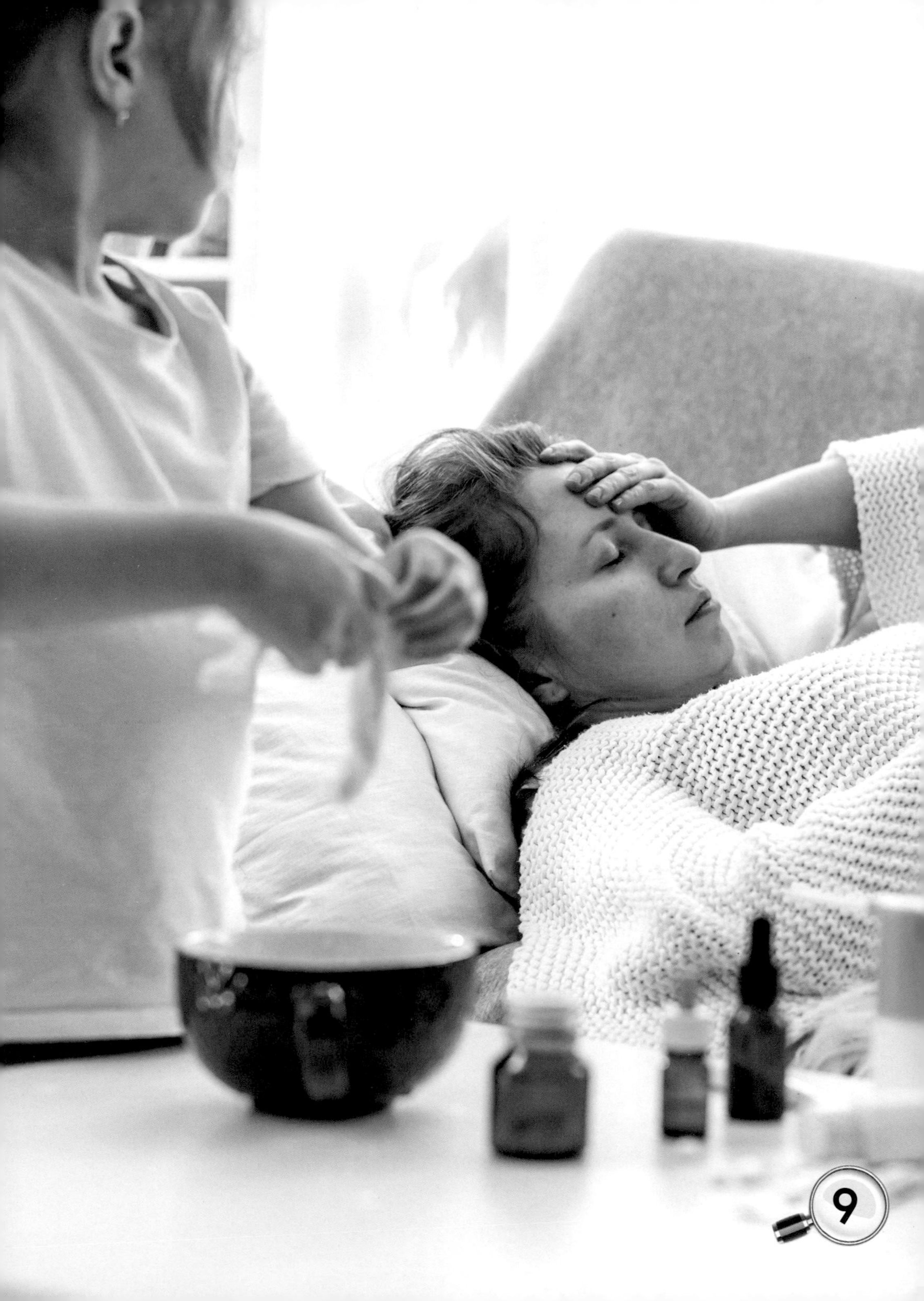

Germs can make me sick, too!

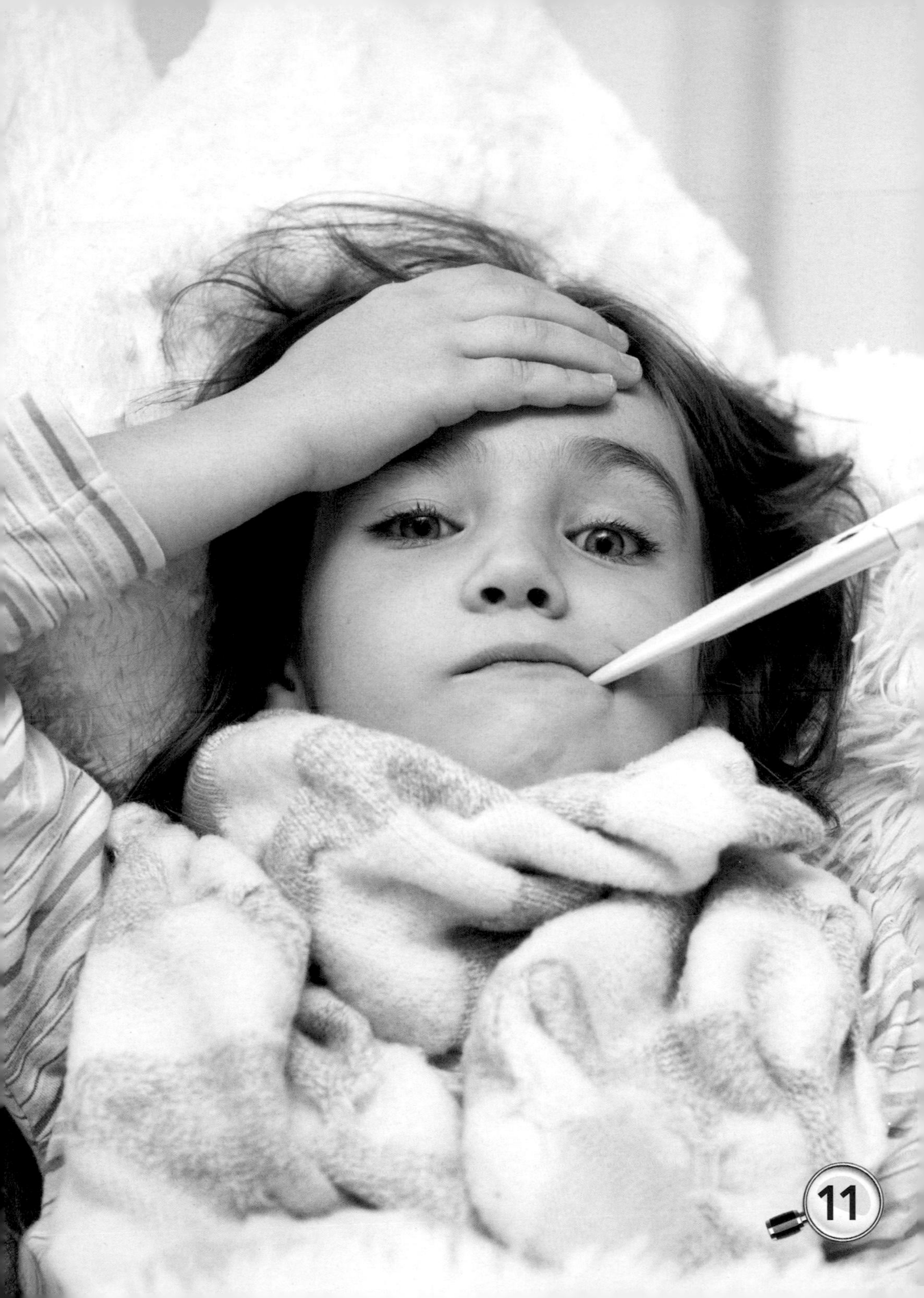

I can wash
my hands here.

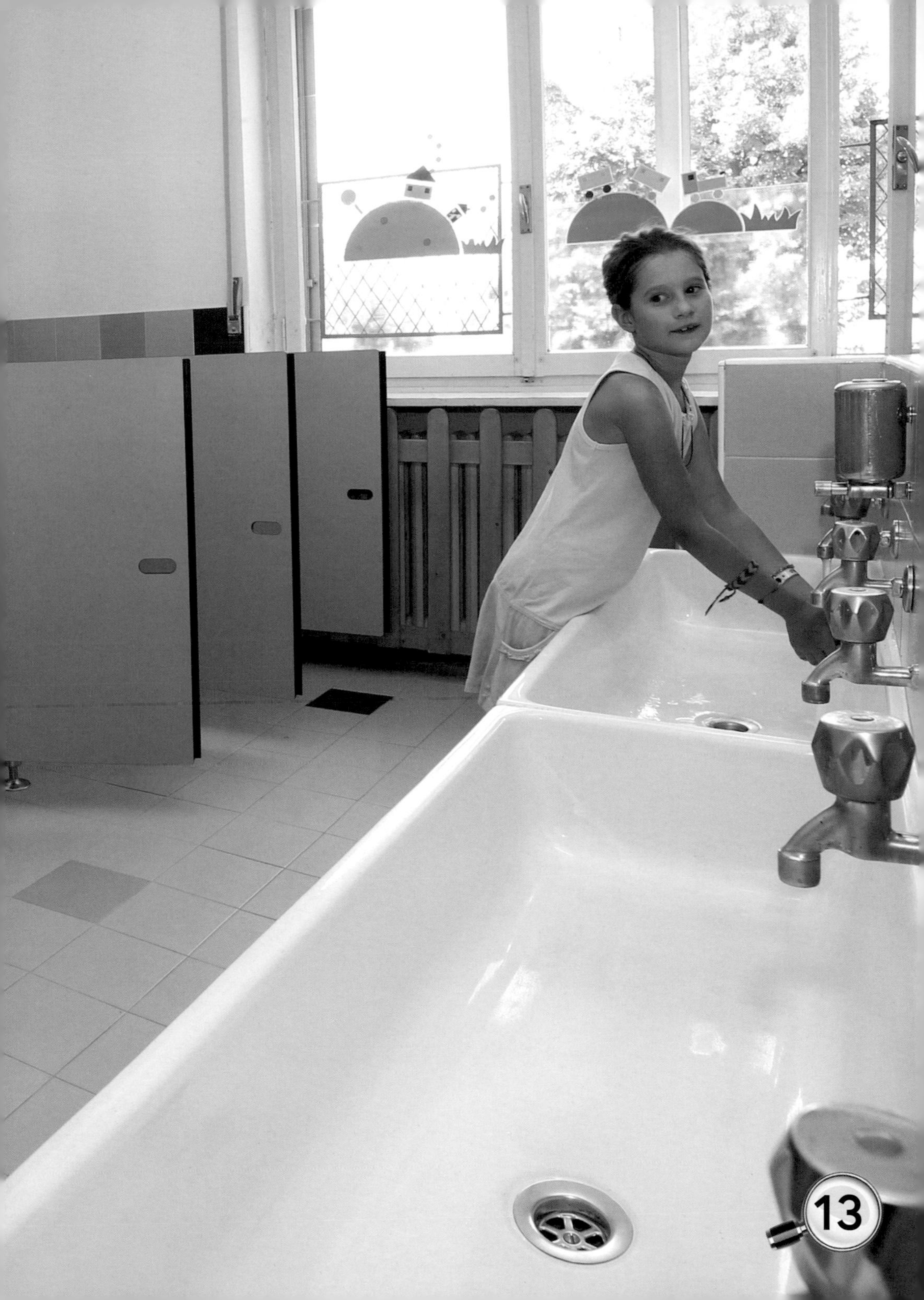

I can wash
my hands here, too!

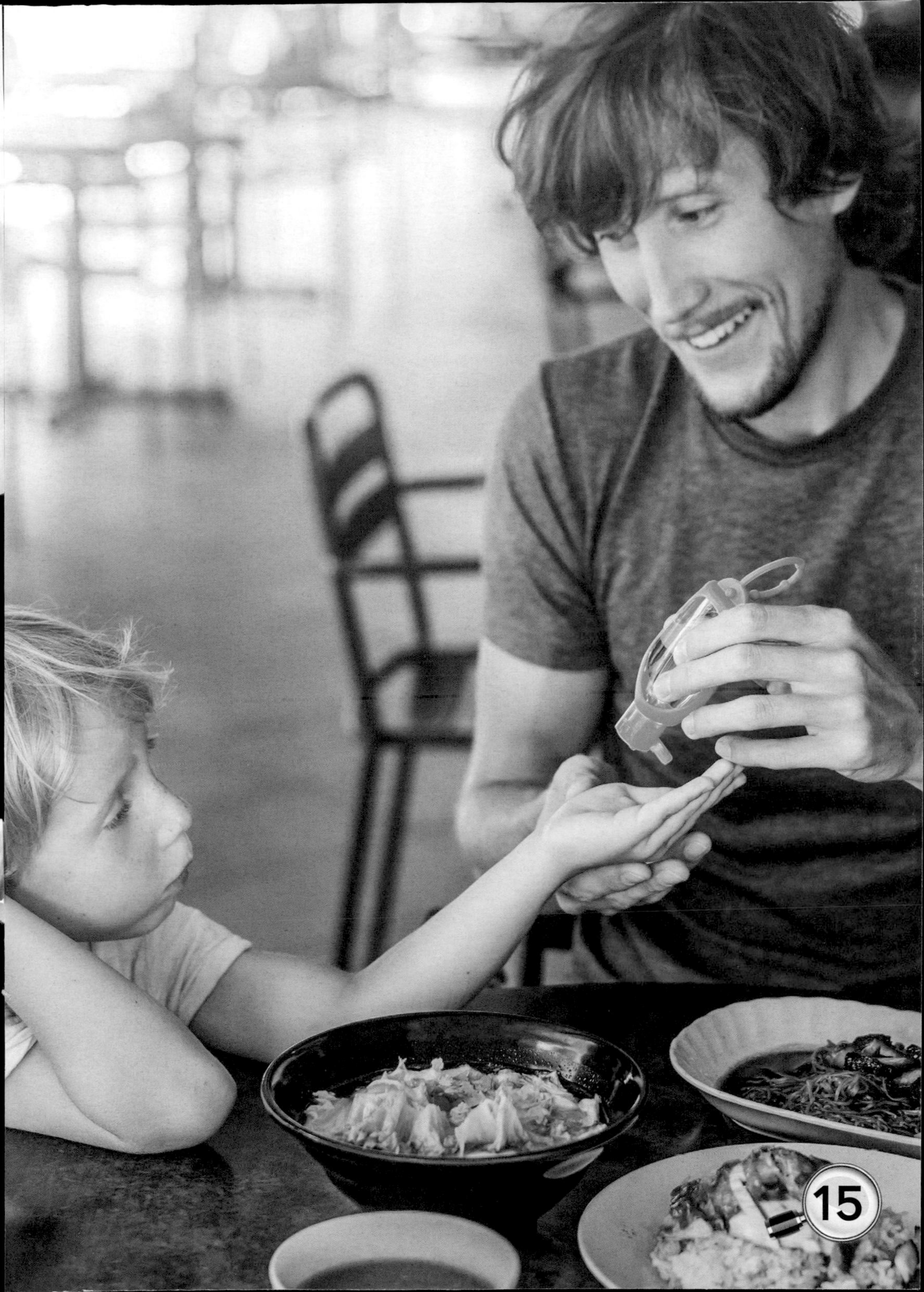

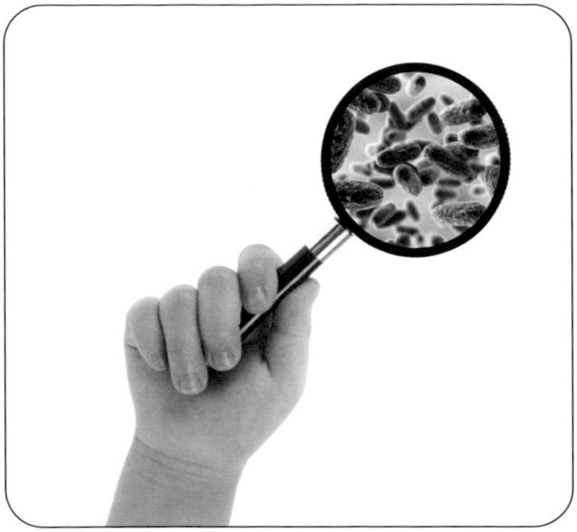

germs

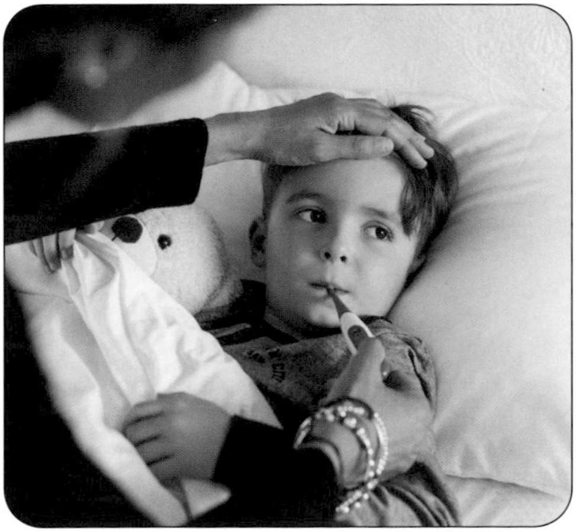

sick